# THE PRESIDENT'S STUCK IN THE BATHTUB

## POEMS ABOUT THE PRESIDENTS

★ *by Susan Katz* ★ *Illustrated by Robert Neubecker* ★

**CLARION BOOKS**

Houghton Mifflin Harcourt ★ Boston New York 2012

Clarion Books
215 Park Avenue South
New York, New York 10003

Clarion Books is an imprint of Houghton Mifflin Harcourt Publishing Company.

www.hmhbooks.com

The illustrations in this book were done in India ink with digital color.
The text was set in 13-point Bodoni Classic.

Library of Congress Cataloging-in-Publication Data
Katz, Susan.
The president's stuck in the bathtub : poems about U.S. presidents / written by Susan Katz ; illustrated by Robert Neubecker.
p. cm.
ISBN 978-0-547-18221-6
1. Presidents—United States—Juvenile poetry. 2. Children's poetry, American. I. Neubecker, Robert, ill. II. Title.
PS3561.A775P74 2012
811'.54—dc22
2011009640

Manufactured in China.
LEO 10 9 8 7 6 5 4 3 2 1
4500322735

For Megan Davis Tarangelo, with love
—S.K.

To Dr. Ruthie
—R.N.

# ★ CONTENTS ★

# Where Didn't George Washington Sleep?

(George Washington, 1789–97)

George Washington slept at Charles Polk's, Dr. Brown's, Appleby's,
Widow Ramsey's, Governor Sharp's, Judge Bee's.
And his own house, the White House—he must have slept there. I'll check.

I know he slept at Hog Island Ferry, Fishkill, Swan Point,
Turkey Foot, Eagle's Nest, Frog's Neck, Oyster Bay,
Orangetown, Red Bank—and the White House? Just a sec.

For sure he slept at Washington's Mill, Barren Hill, Beltsville,
Port Tobacco, Pomfret, Whippany, Parsippany,
Murdering Town, Nicetown, Hobb's Hole, Hackensack.

But did he sleep at the White House? Not once—and that's a fact.

As a surveyor and military man, **George Washington** often traveled. His diaries and letters mention more than 1,000 places where he spent the night. The White House (known in Washington's day as the President's House) took so long to build, however, that Washington, who chose the site and the architects, died before the building was finished, three years after John Adams suceeded him.

# His Majesty, the President
(John Adams, 1797–1801)

John Adams thought presidents should be
graced by the title "His Majesty."
The senators thought this title too fancy
and, for a democracy, rather chancy.
But Adams wouldn't stop talking about it,
no matter how much the Senate might doubt it.
One senator, tired of hearing him drone,
gave Adams a title of his own,
"His Rotundity," for Adams was plump,
amply padded from stomach to rump.
Though Adams bewailed this embarrassing fate,
at least his new title carried some weight.

The mocking title given to **John Adams** by Senator Ralph Izard may be the first instance of mudslinging in American politics. Although it was during George Washington's tenure that Adams argued in favor of the title "His Majesty, the President," Adams's opponents still called him "His Rotundity" during his own term in office.

# Decisions, Decisions

(Thomas Jefferson, 1801–9)

Thomas Jefferson designed

a rope apparatus that shifted his bed
    up to the ceiling
or down to the floor;

a two-faced clock that he could see
    inside the house
or outside the house;

a swivel chair so he could swirl
    to his right
or to his left;

a dumbwaiter that hauled his drinks
    down to the cellar
or back upstairs;

a door on a pivot that he could swing
    open to the dining room
or open to the passage;

a revolving stand so he could read
    five books
    at one time.

A cleverer man you couldn't find,
    but somewhat unable
to make up his mind.

**Thomas Jefferson** played a role in the design of many inventions, often improving upon other people's ideas. His contributions included an octagonal house, a polygraph machine for writing several copies of a letter simultaneously, a ladder that folded up into a pole, and a wheel cipher for using secret codes (a version of which was used until World War II, nearly a century and a half later).

# A Presidential Morsel

(James Madison, 1809–17)

Some presidents
were tall,
with lanky legs
and great strides.
James Madison
was small.

Some presidents
were big,
heavy as boulders
and thick as trees.
James Madison
was a twig.

Some presidents
owned fierce pets
like lions, alligators,
tigers, and bears.
James Madison
owned a parrot.

Had *his* pet
been large
and quick to attack,
James Madison
might have become
the First Snack.

**James Madison,** sometimes referred to as "the Great Little Madison," weighed barely one hundred pounds and stood about five feet, four inches tall. Many presidents received exotic animals as gifts. Herbert Hoover's son Allan kept alligators in the White House, and Thomas Jefferson kept caged grizzly bears on the White House lawn. Generally, however, unusual pets were donated to the National Zoo.

# A White House Visit
(James Monroe, 1817–25)

On an afternoon he would long remember,
William Crawford, a cabinet member,
paid James Monroe a social call
that almost became a White House brawl.
Crawford shouted and shook his stick,
but the president was very quick.
He hoisted the fireplace tongs with a heave,
and then William Crawford decided to leave.

William H. Crawford, the secretary of the Treasury, had a long history of political disagreements with **James Monroe.** On this occasion, as soon as Monroe shouted and grabbed the tongs, Crawford left in a hurry. He never visited President Monroe again.

# The Naked Truth

(John Quincy Adams, 1825–29)

John Quincy Adams would hike
to the river at dawn,
hanging pantaloons, shirt,
and underwear
from the limbs of a handy sycamore.
He liked to swim without them.

But once he couldn't find his clothes.
So, wearing nothing
but water from collar to toes,
he sat on a rock
and waited till his servant
brought him something to wear.

John Quincy didn't care.
Nakedness suited him fine.
Whether rockbound
or swimming against the tide,
this president
    had nothing to hide.

**John Quincy Adams's** skinny-dipping in the Potomac was well known. He was even spotted wearing nothing except goggles and a swim cap by the British minister to Washington. Adams is rumored to have lost his clothing several times because it either fell into the river or was stolen by boys. And it's certain that on June 13, 1825, he had to sit on a rock for five or six hours, waiting for a new outfit, before he could return to the White House.

# Spelling Be

(Andrew Jackson, 1829–37)

Andrew Jackson, some people claim,
was barely able to spell his own name.
He was never the champ of a spelling bee,
never the one to spell "Miss-iss-ipp-i."
Yet he kept the Congress under his thumb.
He couldn't spel rite, but he wasn't dum.

**Andrew Jackson** was one of our strongest presidents, using his forceful personality to expand the powers of the presidency. Though he couldn't master the spelling of even a simple word such as *bugs* (which he spelled "buggs"), this problem didn't disturb him. In fact, he's reported to have claimed that a person who could spell a word only one way lacked imagination.

# The President's O.K.

## (Martin Van Buren, 1837–41)

*Martin Van Buren!*

       *Martin Van Buren!*

The name was too long for crowds to cheer.

So . . .

     they gave him a nickname:

*The Little Magician!*

       *The Little Magician!*

(That was longer still—oh, dear.)

So . . .

     they gave him another:

*Old Kinderhook!*

      *Old Kinderhook!*

(That didn't make much of a buzz.)

So . . .

     they shortened it:

*O.K.!*

   *O.K.!*

      (And indeed it was!)

**Martin Van Buren's** nickname "The Little Magician" referred to his political cleverness, and "Old Kinderhook," soon abbreviated as "O.K.," was a reference to his home in Kinderhook, New York. No one's sure where the word *OK,* meaning "fine," originated. Some people say it was derived from "oll korrect," which was rumored to be Andrew Jackson's spelling of "all correct." But Martin Van Buren gets credit for making the word popular.

## The Long and the Short of It
(William Henry Harrison, 1841)

Without a hat or gloves or overcoat,
William Henry Harrison stood in driving rain
on the Capitol's east steps to declaim to a crowd
the longest, most meandering inaugural address
of any president in history, 3800 words or so,
that took almost two hours to deliver. That was long.

Harrison
was only
president
one month.

That
was
short.

**William Henry Harrison's** election campaign was longer than his
presidency. He caught a cold at his inauguration and a month
later died of pneumonia.

# A Party for the President
(John Tyler, 1841–45)

John Tyler's political party,
                    the Whigs,
met on Capitol Square
                    to expel him.
They called him names,
                    threw stones
at the White House,
                    and fired guns.
Poor Tyler became the president
                    without a party.

When Tyler left office,
                    his wife
hosted the grandest ball
                    ever seen,
with thousands of guests,
                    champagne,
the Marine Band,
                    and candlelight.
Dancing and laughing, Tyler claimed
                    that now he had a party!

By following his own personal beliefs instead of the interests of his political party, **John Tyler** so angered the Whigs that they unanimously voted to oust him. But at his dazzling farewell ball, he announced to departing guests that no one could any longer call him the president without a party.

# How the West Was Won

(James K. Polk, 1845–49)

When James Polk ran for president,
It didn't matter where he went.
He was a nobody nationwide.
"Who is *Polk?*" the voters cried.

But they elected him anyway.
And as president, from his starting day,
Polk yearned for America to grow.
So he laid a claim to Idaho,

Nevada, Wyoming, New Mexico,
Arizona, Texas—and all the rest
Of the places cowboys loved the best.
Polk was the man who won the West.

He thereby showed those doubting folk
Who he was: a real cow-Polk.

**James K. Polk** was the first "dark horse" candidate for the presidency, a man with no national reputation. But as president he added to the country more than a million square miles, which encompasses most of the land in our present-day western states.

# Overdue Mail

(Zachary Taylor, 1849–50)

The Whigs have nominated you
for president,
the letter sent
to Zachary Taylor said.
But the Whigs
mailed it
         postage due.

Taylor didn't want to spend
ten cents,
so he refused that mail,
dispatched it
back to the dead
letter office.
         There it sat.

After waiting
for quite some time,
the Whigs decided to invest
a dime
for a second letter,
postage paid.
         That worked better.

Taylor happily agreed
and led the Whigs
to victory,
the only man in either camp
who won
the presidency
         by a stamp.

In **Zachary Taylor's** time, sending mail with the postage unpaid was a common practice. But Taylor had received so many postage-due letters that he refused to accept any more of them. Most sources say it took several weeks for the Whigs to realize what had happened. When they sent him a second, prepaid notification letter, he accepted immediately.

# Forgotten
(Millard Fillmore, 1850–53)

Poor Millard Fillmore
is always forgotten;
they call him obscure.
Isn't that rotten?

It isn't his fault
that he didn't fill more
than a speck in our country's
records and lore.

Perhaps what he needs
is a story or song,
so here is a poem
to help him along.

A poem to grant him
his moment in history,
redeem him from silence,
darkness, and mystery.

A poem to make
all the world cheer and shout.
A poem—but wait.
*Who's* this poem about?

Vice president under Zachary Taylor, **Millard Fillmore** rose to the presidency when Taylor unexpectedly died. Fillmore spent only two and a half years in office before he failed in a bid to become his party's presidential candidate for the next election. Then he sank back into obscurity.

# O Christmas Tree!
## (Franklin Pierce, 1853–57)

President Pierce trimmed
the first White House tree
for Sunday School children,
who viewed it with glee.
This holiday gesture
won Pierce much applause
and perhaps a vote—
from Santa Claus.

**Franklin Pierce** was the first president to decorate a Christmas tree in the White House. The Christmas tree–lighting ceremony on the White House lawn, a tradition that still continues, began in 1923 under President Calvin Coolidge. In 1954 President Dwight D. Eisenhower added a Pathway of Peace with fifty-six smaller trees, representing fifty states, five territories, and the District of Columbia. Today all fifty-seven trees are lit each evening during the last three weeks of December.

# Funny-Looking
## (James Buchanan, 1857–61)

With one eye, James Buchanan saw far;
with the other eye, he saw near.
So he cocked his head to focus.
He could tilt his view toward a distant star,
ogle an ash on a nearby cigar,
or peer halfway to Zanzibar.
Was there anything he didn't notice?
He could count the bulbs on the chandelier,
discover a flea in someone's ear,
or scrutinize the atmosphere.
What optical hocus-pocus!

**James Buchanan's** habit of tilting his head to the side to favor one eye or the other was echoed, oddly enough, by the behavior of his dog, Lara, who had the habit of lying for hours with one eye closed and one eye open.

# Hatbox
## (Abraham Lincoln, 1861–65)

Abraham Lincoln wore
a hat as tall and skinny
as he was.   More than
ornament for his head,
this president used his
hat instead for carrying
papers—his letters, bills,
or legal documents like
wills. Messy fragments
spilled everywhere, his
written scraps tumbling
over his hair.  Wasn't it
apt—for  thoughts that set the world
ablaze to be stored in a stovepipe hat!

To avoid losing his papers, **Abraham Lincoln** stuffed them into his hat. A story is told that he once bought a new hat and forgot to answer a letter because he'd left it in his old hat. When Lincoln's actual stovepipe hat was sent to Chicago for an exhibit of Lincoln artifacts in 1997, it was considered so valuable that it arrived not only carefully padded and crated but accompanied by an armed escort.

# The President's Bargain
(Andrew Johnson, 1865–69)

Andrew Johnson bought Alaska.
Seward, his negotiator,
paid about two cents an acre.
But folks who disliked cold and ice
protested paying such a price
for a giant refrigerator.
They called Alaska "Seward's folly,"
making poor Johnson melancholy—
until, at last, in a grand finale,
gold was found in Alaskan earth,
and the president got his two cents' worth.

The secretary of state William Seward signed a treaty with Russia by which the United States bought Alaska for $7,200,000. Though people at the time vigorously disapproved, today the Alaska Purchase is considered by many the highest achievement of **Andrew Johnson's** presidency and one of the great accomplishments in U.S. history.

# Out Hunting
## (Ulysses S. Grant, 1869–77)

Hunting wild turkeys,
Ulysses Grant remembered
to stalk silently,
to hide carefully, deep
in the trees.
When two, three,
or twenty handsome turkeys
thundered by,
not one
escaped his eye.
Grant remembered
to watch where they flew,
but there was one thing
he forgot to do.
Oh, shoot!
Yet by keeping his gun
propped on his shoulder,
he gave those birds
a shot
at growing older.

Persuaded once to go turkey hunting with friends, **Ulysses S. Grant** was so fascinated by watching the turkeys fly that he never thought to aim his gun at them. Although Grant, as a general, was responsible for leading his men into some of the bloodiest battles in U.S. history, he was unusually gentle with animals and children. As a boy, he couldn't bear working in his father's tannery, where animal hides were made into leather, and all his life he hated the sight of blood so much that he wouldn't even eat rare meat.

# The President's on the Phone
(Rutherford B. Hayes, 1877–81)

Rutherford B. Hayes
                    got a telephone
              before almost anyone.
                    So everyone
              in Washington
        could remember his phone
                    number:  ONE.

              With his telephone
Rutherford B. Hayes
                         truly shone,
                         for none
              could deny he won
the right to say
                    he was the one
        and only
                         Number One.

When **Rutherford B. Hayes** had the first telephone installed
in the White House, the invention was so new that there were
almost no other phones in Washington. A phone line was set
up connecting the White House to the Treasury Department,
but when a quartet of Hayes's friends sang a song over this
line, one of them hit a high C and shattered the telephone's
sounding board.

# Captain Garfield

(James A. Garfield, 1881)

James Garfield never dreamed he was meant
to become a U.S. president.
His dream was to sail the seven seas.
So he read about bowsprits, mizzen masts, galleys,
bilge pumps, belaying pins—all he could learn.
He sailed through the library full speed astern.
But since what he knew about heaving the hook
or bearing to starboard came from a book,
when he actually went to the shipping dock,
he was in for an unexpected shock.
They told him he wasn't at all the sort
to buffet the waves or lie athwart.
His maritime dreams had run aground,
and suddenly he was homeward-bound.
Barred from the world of sea dogs and ships,
he finally settled for politics.
Spending his time reading books once again,
he soon was the most well-informed congressman,
which led him, at last, to a nautical fate
as the captain of our ship of state.

Unfortunately **James A. Garfield** served as president for only four months before he was shot by an assassin. But during his earlier political career, he spent more time in the Library of Congress than any other congressman and became known as an expert on many topics. Other presidents were also avid readers. Harry S. Truman, as a boy, read every book in his hometown library. Theodore Roosevelt read at least a book a day. John F. Kennedy and Jimmy Carter were both speed readers, tearing through books at the rate of two thousand words per minute.

# "Hail to the Chief"
## (Chester A. Arthur, 1881–85)

Our official presidential theme
made Chester Arthur want to scream.
Its entire history was terribly wrong.
First it began as a boating song,
which gave Chester Arthur a sinking feeling.
But the problem that really sent him reeling
was the fact that this ballad, to Arthur's dismay,
had been sung on the stage in a musical play
called *The Lady of the Lake.*
That was more than he could take.

He spoke to musician John Philip Sousa
and told him how desperately we could use a
new song. With that, the subject was closed,
and President Arthur felt much more composed.
So that's how our country's official motif
was changed from the former "Hail to the Chief"
to the famed "Presidential Polonaise,"
which became so beloved it lasted for . . . days.

"Hail to the Chief" was first used to honor the president during John Tyler's term in office. Then James K. Polk's wife requested that it be played regularly to announce the president's arrival, since Polk was so short that no one noticed when he entered a room. The new song that the composer John Philip Sousa wrote for **Chester A. Arthur** lasted for a few hundred days, but "Hail to the Chief" was restored by Grover Cleveland (though it briefly disappeared again under Gerald R. Ford, who chose to substitute for it the University of Michigan's fight song).

# Double Take

## (Grover Cleveland, 1885–89, 1893–97)

Who was president twenty-two?
Grover Cleveland, that's who.
And who was president twenty-four?
Grover Cleveland once more.
Defeated by president twenty-three,
did Grover Cleveland quit? Not he!
One of the most determined of men,
he stood right up and tried again.
The reward for this resolve was immense:
Cleveland gets counted as *two* presidents.

As First Lady Frances Cleveland departed the White House in 1889 after Benjamin Harrison's defeat of her husband, she instructed the White House staff to take good care of things because the Clevelands would be back in four years. And indeed they were! **Grover Cleveland,** a man so determined that he was sometimes referred to as "His Obstinacy," ran against Harrison a second time and won, becoming the only president to serve two nonconsecutive terms in office.

# The President Sees the Light

(Benjamin Harrison, 1889–93)

In 1891,
the president,
Benjamin Harrison,
ordered electric
lights in the
White
House.

But he
would let the
lights burn the whole
night long unless
a bold servant
doused
them.

It seems
the president
was too scared to
flick the switches
from on to off.
What a
shock!

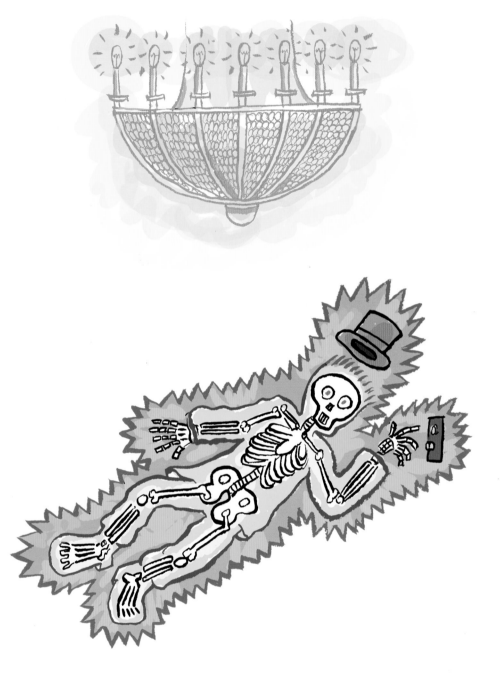

**Benjamin Harrison,** grandson of President William Henry Harrison, was so afraid of getting an electric shock that he asked Ike Hoover, one of the electricians, to remain at the White House to turn the lights on and off. Hoover liked being there so well that he stayed and worked as a White House aide for more than forty years.

# Yankee Doodle Dandy
## (William McKinley, 1897–1901)

This president taught his parrot
the tune to "Yankee Doodle."
McKinley would whistle the opening bar,
then let the parrot be the star
and finish up the rest.

But the president never taught him the words.
Perhaps he thought it best
not to mention the feather in Doodle's hat,
for what would a parrot think of that?
He might not consider it dandy.

**William McKinley's** parrot
was named Washington Post.
He talked to everyone who passed his
cage, which hung in a prominent place
in the White House. Another talkative
presidential parrot was Andrew Jackson's
Poll. At Jackson's funeral service, the bird
had to be carried out because he wouldn't stop
screeching swear words.

# The White House Gang
(Theodore Roosevelt, 1901–9)

A member of the White House Gang,
started by Quentin Roosevelt,
had to be brave enough to swallow
ooey gooey fish eyes
or chew a three-inch worm
for the world's longest minute
(blindfolded so he couldn't tell
it was only tapioca or spaghetti).
A member of the White House Gang
might get the Hot Hand,
a smack with a shingle on his behind
so he couldn't sit down for a year.
Or the White Hand,
a sack of flour rub-a-scrub-dubbed
into his hair and sifted
down his neck so it itched forever.
Or the Black Hand,
a mouthful of fireplace soot
that darkened his spit for life.
He might be forced
to jump from the roof balustrade,
wallop his head on the marble floor,
or be dragged down the stairs by his feet.
The only boys bold enough to join
were Taffy, Sailor, Walker, Slats,
Bromley, Look, and Q.
Oh, yes, and the president too.

Quentin Roosevelt, nicknamed "Q" by his friends, was the youngest of **Theodore Roosevelt's** six lively children. Quentin filled the White House with a group of boys who became known as the White House Gang. The president, an honorary member, often joined the gang in pillow fights and other rough-and-tumble games.

# The President's Stuck in the Bathtub

(William Howard Taft, 1909–13)

In the midst of his bath,
Poor President Taft
Discovered the tub didn't fit him.
In fact, he got stuck.
(What horrible luck!)
Taft filled up the tub to the brim.

When he gave a loud shout,
People hoisted him out
By tugging him here and there.
Then they built a new tub
In which four men could scrub
(Though I doubt that Taft wanted to share.)

Singing *rub-a-dub-dub*,
Taft enjoyed his grand tub.
There was never a further commotion.
Despite his great weight,
I'm pleased to relate,
He stayed safe in his own private ocean.

At his largest, **William Howard Taft** weighed around 350 pounds. The four workers who installed his new bathtub were photographed all sitting in it together. Ironically, when Harry S. Truman was living in the White House, his bathtub (a normal-size one) began to sink as he was taking a bath one day, and the Trumans had to move out while the White House was repaired.

# Baaad Sheep
## (Woodrow Wilson, 1913–21)

President Wilson wished to keep
On the lawn of the White House his own flock of sheep.

He believed his new pets would mow all the grass,
But that's not exactly what came to pass.

You wouldn't be getting it wrong if you said
That they cropped and gobbled the shrubs instead.

Bushes for breakfast and hedges for lunch—
There weren't any limits to what they would munch.

Though President Wilson achieved his fond wish,
He ended up feeling a tiny bit sheepish.

**Woodrow Wilson's** sheep grazed on the South Lawn of the White House during World War I. The leader of the flock, Old Ike, was famous for chewing tobacco. The wool from the Wilsons' sheep, sold at a special auction, raised more than $50,000 for the Red Cross.

# Would You Repeat That?
(Warren G. Harding, 1921–23)

Always an admirer of alliteration,
Harding hardly ever halted his habit of haranguing
crowds by constantly copying compatible consonants.
This pretentious passion for pompous palaver produced
a superfluity of sonorous syllables, sounding spectacular
except that nobody ever knew what he said.

Tall and handsome, with a mesmerizing voice, **Warren G. Harding** drew crowds
to his public appearances even though his speeches were often incomprehensi-
ble. H. L. Mencken, a famous newspaper columnist of the time, said Harding's
oratory reminded him of "a string of wet sponges."

# A Penny for Your Thoughts
## (Calvin Coolidge, 1923–29)

President Coolidge was quiet.
Conversation with him
was a solo,
  never a duet.

And then one evening at dinner,
the lady beside him said,
"You *have* to talk to me."

Coolidge chewed his bread.

Leaning closer, the lady insisted,
"I've made a bet
with some of my friends
  that I could get
more than two words out of you."

The president didn't think twice.
His reply was highly concise:

  "You lose."

Though **Calvin Coolidge's** refusal to engage in small talk won him the nickname "Silent Cal," he actually did more public speaking than most presidents, holding 520 press conferences and giving more speeches than any of his predecessors.

# Lost in Translation

(Herbert Hoover, 1929–33)

In crowds, since he hated to be overheard,
This president wouldn't use one English word.
He spoke to his wife in Chinese instead.
It's disturbing to think what they might have said.
*Your zipper's unzipped. You ate too much bread.*
*Your corset's too tight, and you're turning red.*
*That gentleman looks like a shrunken head.*
The possibilities fill one with dread.

Imagine them saying whatever they pleased:
*Did that man wipe his nose with his tie when he sneezed?*
*That lady is scratching. I bet she has fleas.*
*These folks are such windbags, I'm feeling a breeze.*
*This caviar tastes just like antifreeze.*
The Hoovers kept secrets with such total ease,
It might incline others to study Chinese.

When Lou and **Herbert Hoover** were first married, they lived in China, where Mrs. Hoover learned to speak fluent Mandarin. Though the president knew only about a hundred Chinese words, he kept those words fresh in his mind by using them for secret conversations.

# A Dog's Life

## (Franklin D. Roosevelt, 1933–45)

Franklin Roosevelt's Scottish terrier, Fala,
joined the army as an honorary private,
conferred with England's prime minister,
and helped to inspect defense plants.

Dignitaries waited for their dinner
till Roosevelt finished feeding the dog.
And every morning a bone for Fala
arrived on the president's breakfast tray.

The Scottie slept beside Roosevelt's bed,
had his own secretary to handle his mail,
and was constantly hounded by the press.
One joker suggested the dog should run for office.

But though Fala even starred in films
and received more fan mail than Roosevelt,
still the president never allowed
the country to go to the dogs.

**Franklin D. Roosevelt's** Fala was given the Secret Service code name "The Informer" because the president took him along on top-secret train trips; at every station, the combination of a curtained train and a Secret Service man walking the famous Scottie was a dead giveaway of the president's whereabouts. Today a three-foot statue of Fala rests beside the president's statue in the FDR Memorial in Washington, D.C.

# A Haunting Story
(Harry S. Truman, 1945–53)

One night in the White House, left all on his own,
Harry Truman discovered he wasn't alone.
Three sharp raps on his bedroom door
made him spring awake in the midst of a snore.
Feet paced the hallway; curtain rods shook.
He put on his glasses to take a good look,
but all he could see was unoccupied air.
Nobody, *nada,* nothing was there.
At that very moment, he claimed he could sense
the ghostly presence of dead presidents.
Though he probably wanted to run down the hall,
he refused to react to the ghosts at all.
But his tale might give some folks a bit of a scare,
for if it is true, then Truman's still there.

People differ about how serious **Harry S. Truman** was when he said the White House was "haunted, sure as shootin'," but previous White House residents and visitors had also claimed to have encountered ghosts. During Truman's second term, however, the White House underwent total reconstruction, and since that renovation, fewer ghosts have been reported there.

# Liking Ike
## (Dwight D. Eisenhower, 1953–61)

Though Eisenhower's name was Dwight,
he used for his slogan his nickname, Ike.
Finding this choice a perfect delight,
people shouted in chorus, "We like Ike!"
Dwight never acknowledged his terrible plight:
He and five brothers were nicknamed alike.
(Dwight hadn't applied for a copyright.)
So I have a question—I hope it's polite—
How did the voters know which one to like,
Ike, Ike, Ike, Ike, Ike, or Ike?

**Dwight D. Eisenhower** was the third of seven brothers, one of whom died in infancy. His surviving brothers—Arthur, Edgar, Roy, Earl, and Milton—were all known, at one time or another, as "Ike," even though their mother, Ida, disapproved of the nickname. In high school, Dwight was sometimes differentiated by being called "Ugly Ike."

# Elevator Operator

(John F. Kennedy, 1961–63)

Tourists thought
    Congressman John Kennedy
      was the elevator boy,
        and they asked him for
          the fourth floor.
            He was surprised,

but those folks had one thing right:

          UP.
        going
    was
He

**John F. Kennedy** was also once mistaken for a page by a fellow congressman. He contributed to his boyish appearance by dressing casually, sometimes wearing khaki pants or sneakers. Though Kennedy, at forty-three, was the youngest president ever elected, he was not the youngest man to serve as president. Theodore Roosevelt, who became president when William McKinley was assassinated, was only forty-two at the time.

# LBJ
(Lyndon B. Johnson, 1963–69)

President
          Lyndon Baines Johnson
had a wife named
          Lady Bird Johnson,
a daughter named
          Lynda Bird Johnson,
a daughter named
          Luci Baines Johnson,
a dog named
          Little Beagle Johnson,
a horse named
          Lady B Johnson,
a nickname,
          Light Bulb Johnson,
and a ranch called
          the LBJ.
When his fans chanted
          "LBJ
all the way!"
          they weren't kidding.

**Lyndon B. Johnson** earned his nickname by walking through the White House every night, turning off the lights to save taxpayer money. Mrs. Johnson, whose legal name was Claudia, received her nickname at the age of two when the family cook called her "purty as a lady bird." The president sometimes joked that his family saved money on luggage by all having the same monogram.

# A Presidential Memo
(Richard M. Nixon, 1969–74)

JANUARY 30, 1969     2:02 a.m.
TO: **Mrs. Nixon**
FROM: **The President**

With regard to President RN, I have several items to recommend:

When I waken from my slumber in the middle of the night,
I require double dictaphones on a table to my right.
To facilitate a fire blazing brightly in July,
I request the air conditioner be set to extra high.
I advise some alterations to the bathroom shower stall
since the current water pressure pins me to the wall.

Some wives might not read memos, but you're always a good sport,
so I trust that you will follow up and send me a report.

**Richard M. Nixon** loved to write memos to everyone, even his family. The items mentioned in this poem are factual. Nixon often got up in the middle of the night to put his thoughts on tape. In summer he liked to work beside a blazing fire with the air conditioner turned the whole way up. And the special high-pressure shower Lyndon B. Johnson had installed in the White House nearly blasted Nixon out of the bathroom.

# President What's-His-Name
(Gerald R. Ford, 1974–77)

When he was born,
Gerald Ford was named for his father,
Leslie Lynch King.

When he learned to walk
and learned to talk,
he was Leslie Lynch King, Junior.

Before he was five,
he was renamed for his stepfather,
Gerald Rudolph Ford.

Without that change,
one of America's presidents
would have been a King.

In childhood, both before and after his parents' divorce and his mother's remarriage, **Gerald R. Ford** was actually called "Junie," for Junior. Ford's name change was the most drastic of any president's, but six other presidents—Grant, Cleveland, Wilson, Coolidge, Eisenhower, and Clinton—also changed their names.

# President Attacked by Rabbit
## (Jimmy Carter, 1977–81)

Jimmy Carter fished on his pond.
The day was fair, the water calm,
When suddenly nearby something splashed.
Nostrils flared. Teeth flashed.
And through the water a creature flew,
Heading straight for Carter's canoe.

Sometimes a story's not what it appears.
In fact, this attacker had very long ears,
Enormous brown eyes, and a cotton tail—
A nibbler of lettuce, carrots, and kale.
Yet it seemed positively determined to chew
A rabbit-size serving of fisherman stew.
It panted and pawed to climb into the boat
As the president struggled to stay afloat.
He splashed that rabbit aft and fore
Till it finally turned and swam for shore.

One part of this story makes me nervous.
Where on earth was the Secret Service?
Those folks who'd have fearlessly wrestled Jaws
Lacked a clue how to handle a villain with paws.
So this is the truth: you can bet your money
No one's prepared for a killer bunny.

**Jimmy Carter** encountered the "swamp rabbit" at a pond on his farm in Plains, Georgia. The story made front-page news in the *Washington Post,* under the headline "President Attacked by Rabbit." The accompanying picture was a poster from the movie *Jaws,* showing a rabbit instead of a shark and headed "Paws."

★ 51

# Madame Mitterrand Wouldn't Move

## (Ronald Reagan, 1981–89)

As Ronald Reagan led her to dinner,
Madame Mitterrand suddenly stopped.
The butler motioned for her to come,
But Madame Mitterrand wouldn't move.
The president gently tugged on her arm,
But Madame Mitterrand wouldn't move.
He whispered that they were supposed to go,
But Madame Mitterrand wouldn't move.
Though she whispered back to him in French,
Madame Mitterrand still wouldn't move.
Her interpreter finally ran up to confess,
"Mr. President, your foot's on her dress."

**Ronald Reagan's** uncooperative dinner partner was the wife of the French president François Mitterrand, who was guest of honor at a state dinner. Reagan wasn't the only president to suffer embarrassment on his way to a formal White House meal. John F. Kennedy once graciously ushered the Danish prime minister into the butler's pantry instead of the dining room.

# Vegetating
## (George H. W. Bush, 1989–93)

George Bush hated broccoli when he was a kid,
And so, as our president, here's what he did:
While meeting the press, he announced with glee
That broccoli was now his declared enemy.
He rebelled against broccoli—he wouldn't give ground,
He'd not have one ounce of that veggie around.
Not a stalk, not a leaf, not a green molecule
On one White House plate under George Bush's rule.
Since he was the chief, he did not have to eat it.
Broccoli was doomed; he was going to defeat it.
How odd to wage war as if broccoli were vicious
When so many folks find it simply delicious.

**George H. W. Bush** banned broccoli not only from the White House menu but from the menu of Air Force One, the presidential jet, as well. In an interview, he compared his rejection of broccoli to Poland's rebellion against the Soviet Union. In protest, broccoli growers shipped to the White House truckloads of the vegetable, which were donated to local food banks. Mrs. Bush responded to the outcry by joking that she would order for the president an all-broccoli dinner, including broccoli ice cream.

# Comeback Kid
## (Bill Clinton, 1993–2001)

Bill Clinton gave a speech so boring
His audience came close to snoring.
The *Tonight Show* host remarked that Bill
Should be approved as a sleeping pill.
Bill could have taken this jest as a blow;
Instead he appeared as a guest on the show
And chuckled over the Clinton jokes
Along with all the other folks.
He even stepped up to the microphone
To tootle a tune on his saxophone.
And perhaps he briefly winked his eye,
For the song he chose was a lullaby.

**Bill Clinton** gave his notorious speech in 1988 to nominate Michael Dukakis as a presidential candidate. Afterward, Clinton joked that his thirty-two minute talk was the longest hour and a half of his life and offered to make a similar speech for Dukakis's opponent. By being able to laugh at himself, Clinton turned an embarrassing failure into an opportunity to actually strengthen his public image.

# Language Terriers
(George W. Bush, 2001–9)

George W. Bush had trouble
with words, using
"terriers" for "barriers," "bariff" for "tariff,"
"plowed" for "proud."

Meaning to say "dreams take wing,"
he said, "wings take dream."
He opposed all "federal cufflinks"
(whatever that might mean).

He spoke of "he and her"
instead of "he and she"
and talked about
a "foreign-handed" foreign policy.

And when he tried to say things once,
they often came out double;
his syllables would cluster
to form a syllabubble.

Some folks found this amusing,
but that seems so unfair!
If he hadn't been the president,
who would ever care?

Attaining highest office
may perhaps be overrated,
for a president's so easily
misunderestimated.

**George W. Bush's** verbal mishaps were often referred to as Bushisms. "Misunder-estimated" is one of the most well-known words that Bush inadvertently coined. He also created proverbs of his own, such as "You can't take the high horse and then claim the low road."

# Yo Mama

## (Barack Obama 2009– )

When Barack Obama launched his campaign,
his opposition made fun of his name.
From the Scotia Sea to Mount Fujiyama,
people came up with a whole panorama
of name after name that was *not* Obama.
He jested that some even called him Yo Mama.

But when voting was over, Obama had won;
he wasn't defeated by wisecrack or pun.
Not a single snicker could anyone vent
at Obama's new name, Mr. President.

When he played high school basketball, **Barack Obama** earned
the nickname "Barry O'Bomber" for his outstanding long jump
shot. And when he visited the Crow reservation in Montana, he
was given the honorary name "Awe kooda bilaxpak kuuxshish,"
which means "one who helps people throughout the land."

# ★ PRESIDENTIAL NOTES AND QUOTES ★

**I. George Washington, 1789–97** (Feb. 22, 1732 – Dec. 14, 1799)

*Liberty, when it begins to take root, is a plant of rapid growth.*

Nickname: "Father of His Country"

— first president pictured on a postage stamp

**2. John Adams, 1797–1801** (Oct. 30, 1735 – July 4, 1826)

*May none but honest and wise men ever rule under this roof.*

Nickname: "Atlas of Independence"

— first president to live in Washington, D.C.

**3. Thomas Jefferson, 1801–9** (April 13, 1743 – July 4, 1826)

*All men are created equal.*

Nickname: "Sage of Monticello"

— first president to shake hands at presidential receptions instead of bowing

**4. James Madison, 1809–17** (Mar. 16, 1751 – June 28, 1836)

*If men were angels, no government would be necessary.*

Nickname: "Father of the Constitution"

— first president to wear long trousers instead of knee breeches

**5. James Monroe, 1817–25** (Apr. 28, 1758 – July 4, 1831)

*The heart of every citizen must expand with joy when he reflects how near our Government has approached to perfection.*

Nickname: "Era-of-Good-Feeling President"

— first president to ride on a steamboat

**6. John Quincy Adams, 1825–29** (July 11, 1767 – Feb. 23, 1848)

*Individual liberty is individual power.*

Nickname: "Old Man Eloquent"

— first president to be photographed

**7. Andrew Jackson, 1829–37** (Mar. 15, 1767 – June 8, 1845)

*One man with courage makes a majority.*

Nickname: "Old Hickory"

— first president to ride on a train

**8. Martin Van Buren, 1837–41** (Dec. 5, 1782 – July 24, 1862)

*The less government interferes with private pursuits the better for the general prosperity.*

Nickname: "The Little Magician"

— first president born an American citizen

**9. William Henry Harrison, 1841** (Feb. 9, 1773 – April 4, 1841)

*Tippecanoe and Tyler too.*

Nickname: "Old Tippecanoe"

— first president to have a campaign slogan

**10. John Tyler, 1841–45** (Mar. 29, 1790 – Jan. 18, 1862)

*I can never consent to being dictated to.*

Nickname: "His Accidency"

— first president to marry while in office

**11. James Knox Polk, 1845–49** (Nov. 2, 1795 – June 15, 1849)

*With me it is emphatically true that the Presidency is no bed of roses.*

Nickname: "Young Hickory"

— first president whose inauguration was reported by telegraph

**12. Zachary Taylor, 1849–50** (Nov. 24, 1784 – July 9, 1850)

*I have always done my duty. I am ready to die. My only regret is for the friends I leave behind me.*

Nickname: "Old Rough and Ready"

— first president never previously elected to any public office

**13. Millard Fillmore, 1850–53** (Jan. 7, 1800 – Mar. 8, 1874)

*May God save the country, for it is evident that the people will not.*

Nickname: "The American Louis Philippe"

— first president to have a stove in the White House instead of a fireplace

**14. Franklin Pierce, 1853–57** (Nov. 23, 1804 – Oct. 8, 1869)

*I wish I could indulge higher hope for the future of our country, but the aspect of any vision is fearfully dark and I cannot make it otherwise.*

Nickname: "Young Hickory of the Granite Hills"

— first president who delivered his inaugural speech from memory

**15. James Buchanan, 1857–61** (Apr. 23, 1791 – June 1, 1868)

*I shall carry to my grave the consciousness that I at least meant well for my country.*

Nickname: "Old Buck"

— first bachelor elected president

**16. Abraham Lincoln, 1861–65** (Feb. 12, 1809 – Apr. 15, 1865)

*With malice toward none, with charity for all.*

Nickname: "Honest Abe"

— first president born outside the boundaries of the thirteen original states (in Kentucky)

**17. Andrew Johnson, 1865–69** (Dec. 29, 1808 – July 31, 1875)

*Honest conviction is my courage; the Constitution is my guide.*

Nickname: "King Andy"

— first president to receive the visit of a queen

**18. Ulysses Simpson Grant, 1869–77** (Apr. 27, 1822 – July 23, 1885)

*There are but few important events in the affairs of men brought about by their own choice.*

Nickname: "Hero of Appomattox"

— first president to establish a national park

**19. Rutherford Birchard Hayes, 1877–81** (Oct. 4, 1822 – Jan. 17, 1893)

*He serves his party best who serves the country best.*

Nickname: "Dark-Horse President"

— first president to visit the West Coast

**20. James Abram Garfield, 1881** (Nov. 19, 1831 – Sept. 19, 1881)

*The civil service can never be placed on a satisfactory basis until it is regulated by law.*

Nickname: "Preacher President"

— first left-handed president

**21. Chester Alan Arthur, 1881–85** (Oct. 5, 1829 – Nov. 18, 1886)

*Men may die, but the fabrics of our free institutions remain unshaken.*

Nickname: "The Gentleman Boss"

— first president to have a valet

**22. & 24. Stephen Grover Cleveland, 1885–89, 1893–97** (Mar. 18, 1837 – June 24, 1908)

*I have tried so hard to do right.*

Nickname: "Grover the Good"

— first president to have a child born in the White House

**23. Benjamin Harrison, 1889–93** (Aug. 20, 1833 – Mar. 13, 1901)

*We Americans have no commission from God to police the world.*

Nickname: "Little Ben"

— first president whose grandfather had also been president

**25. William McKinley, 1897–1901** (Jan. 29, 1843 – Sept. 14, 1901)

*War should never be entered upon until every agency of peace has failed.*

Nickname: "Idol of Ohio"

— first president whose inauguration was recorded by a motion picture camera

**26. Theodore Roosevelt, 1901–9** (Oct. 27, 1858 – Jan. 6, 1919)

*Speak softly and carry a big stick.*

Nickname: "Teddy"

— first president to ride in an automobile, submerge in a submarine, and fly in an airplane

**27. William Howard Taft, 1909–13** (Sept. 15, 1857 – Mar. 8, 1930)

*Politics makes me sick.*

Nickname: "Big Bill"

— first president to pitch a ball to open the baseball season

**28. Thomas Woodrow Wilson, 1913–21** (Dec. 28, 1856 – Feb. 3, 1924)

*The world must be made safe for democracy.*

Nickname: "Schoolmaster in Politics"

— first president to have earned a Ph.D.

**29. Warren Gamaliel Harding, 1921–23** (Nov. 2, 1865 – Aug. 2, 1923)

*America's present need is not heroics, but healing; not nostrums, but normalcy; not revolution, but restoration.*

Nickname: "Wobbly Warren"

— first president to broadcast over the radio

**30. John Calvin Coolidge, 1923–29** (July 4, 1872 – Jan. 5, 1933)

*The chief business of the American people is business.*

Nickname: "Silent Cal"

— first president sworn in by a former president (William Howard Taft)

**31. Herbert Clark Hoover, 1929–33** (Aug. 10, 1874 – Oct. 20, 1964)

*Prosperity is just around the corner.*

Nickname: "The Great Engineer"

— first president to have an asteroid named after him

**32. Franklin Delano Roosevelt, 1933–45** (Jan. 30, 1882 – Apr. 12, 1945)

*I pledge you, I pledge myself, to a new deal for the American people.*

Nickname: "FDR"

— first president with a serious physical disability

**33. Harry S. Truman, 1945–53** (May 8, 1884 – Dec. 26, 1972)

*The buck stops here.*

Nickname: "Give 'Em Hell Harry"

— first president with a televised inauguration

**34. Dwight David Eisenhower, 1953–61** (Oct. 14, 1890 – Mar. 28, 1969)

*What counts is not necessarily the size of the dog in the fight—it's the size of the fight in the dog.*

Nickname: "Ike"

— first president of all fifty states

**35. John Fitzgerald Kennedy, 1961–63** (May 29, 1917 – Nov. 22, 1963)

*Ask not what your country can do for you, ask what you can do for your country.*

Nickname: "JFK"

— first president to win a Pulitzer Prize

**36. Lyndon Baines Johnson, 1963–69** (Aug. 27, 1908 – Jan. 22, 1973)

*In each generation—with toil and tears—we have had to earn our heritage again.*

Nickname: "LBJ"

— first president to take the oath of office in an airplane

**37. Richard Milhous Nixon, 1969–74** (Jan. 9, 1913 – April 22, 1994)

*That the way I tried to deal with Watergate was the wrong way is a burden I shall bear for every day of the life that is left to me.*

Nickname: "Tricky Dick"

— first president to attend the launching of a manned spaceflight

**38. Gerald Rudolph Ford, Jr., 1974–77** (July 14, 1913 – Dec. 26, 2006)

*I am acutely aware that you have not elected me as your President by your ballots, and so I ask you to confirm me as your President with your prayers.*

Nickname: "Jerry"

— first president to escape two assassination attempts by women

**39. James Earl Carter, Jr., 1977–81** (Oct. 1, 1924 – )

*We become not a melting pot but a beautiful mosaic. Different people, different beliefs, different yearnings, different hopes, different dreams.*

Nickname: "Jimmy"

— first president born in a hospital

**40. Ronald Wilson Reagan, 1981–89** (Feb. 6, 1911 – June 5, 2004)

*We have every right to dream heroic dreams.*

Nickname: "Dutch"

— first movie actor to become president

**41. George Herbert Walker Bush, 1989–93** (June 12, 1924 – )

*We have closed a chapter of history. The Cold War is over.*

Nickname: "Poppy"

— first president who had survived his plane being shot down in wartime

**42. William Jefferson Clinton, 1993–2001** (Aug. 19, 1946 – )

*There is nothing wrong with America that cannot be cured by what is right with America.*

Nickname: "The Comeback Kid"

— first president to have been a Rhodes Scholar

**43. George Walker Bush, 2001–9** (July 6, 1946 – )

*We will not tire, we will not falter, and we will not fail.*

Nickname: "Dubya"

— first president to install a treadmill on Air Force One

**44. Barack Hussein Obama, 2009–** (Aug. 4, 1961 – )

*What we have achieved gives us hope—the audacity of hope—for what we can and must achieve tomorrow.*

Nickname (in youth): "Barry O'Bomber"

— first president born outside the contiguous United States (in Hawaii)